elsebeth lav

designer's choice
book seventeen
the small things matter collection
photography anders rydell

Pattern translation and technical editing: Carol Rhoades
Graphic design: Anders Rydell, Ingen Konst AB
Printed in Hong Kong

Acknowledgements

A heartfelt thank you to all the wonderful people who helped make this book possible:

Sion Elalouf and the staff at KFI, always encouraging.

The knitters: Gerd Härnvall, Gullevi Ljungström, Helena Norén, Solveig Näslund and Bertil Rejnevi.

The models: Ami, Johanna, Josefin and Signe. In all fairness, we should also mention Curt the bike.

My friend and colleague Cornelia Tuttle Hamilton for all her help with general text checks.

The Designer

Elsebeth Lavold—a leading authority on cable patterns and a skilled and creative designer of beautiful knitwear. World famous for her Viking Knits Project.

The Yarn

The small things in this book are made in Silky Wool, one of them with Bambool decorations. Instructions for the knitted box Borr on page 29.

The Theme

All small projects, wearable or practical, or both. This "bonus accessory" to the tea cozy Tina is just to open your mind to the endless possibilities of knitting.

The Locations

The majority of the photos were taken at the church of Danderyd with its impressive runestone, and at the Ulvsunda Castle in Stockholm.

Introduction

When a book of small projects was suggested to me, I was in for some serious debating with myself. There were a lot of aspects that were appealing, but also some cons. I wanted to do such a book, but could I? Would I be able to come up with a collection of small projects that still kept the traits that I find important, my "designer personality" if you will, and also the ones that make people choose to knit my designs? Well, here's the book.

"Divine inspiration" is not the issue. I truly believe that all people are creative. For someone who designs for a living, it may be that the process is a bit more formalized. It involves the ability to recognize the fruitful ones in a flow of ideas, and the drive and experience to refine a vague idea, a quick pencil sketch, or a "mistake" in a swatch, into a thought-through end result.

Having said that, the coming-up-with-new-ideas part of the job is, at least for me, not a task that can be carried out just any day. There are days when my mind goes completely blank, and I just have to do totally un-creative things, like cleaning the house. Then there are other days, when new ideas come so fast that some of them may even get lost in the traffic jam.

This is why I like to work with themes in my collections. Having a theme as a "thought holder" helps me to focus, and to end up with a collection that is hopefully consistent and coherent as a whole, even if the individual designs can be quite varied. So to do a book where the only "theme" is that the projects should be small was a challenge to my usual MO.

The idea had quite a few strong points, for example the choice of yarn. Not since the first Designer's Choice book have I made a collection using only Silky Wool (well, for the tea cozy *Tina* on p. 54, I have suggested using Bambool for the I-cord decorations, but nobody's perfect). In *The Viking Knits Collection* I didn't have much of a choice, since at the time Silky Wool was my only yarn. Presently there are nine.

I will not put my name on a yarn that is not pleasant to knit with, or one that doesn't have the properties I require. But, as any parent will tell you, even if you love all your children just as much, there is something special about the firstborn (but maybe I'm biased, since I happen to be the firstborn in my family). And it seems that many knitters share my affection for Silky Wool. Using it for an entire collection was like going back to the roots, but at the same time being able to use all the experience I have gained, having knit with the yarn for many years, in some new ways.

This is the first book where I have made designs for Silky Wool where the yarn is held double; Tina is one example. The obvious reason for this choice was to overcome the restrictions that thickness and gauge place on a yarn, but the result was very satisfying.

Another first, made possible by the fact that most of the projects are small and far less expensive than e.g. a sweater, is that I have dared to suggest felting a few of the designs. In my experience, Silky Wool is very well suited for felting, but I have a European washing machine, and they are a bit different from their American counterparts. For one thing, I had no way to test out "transatlantic shrinking". But here I had designs like bags, where shrinking was not a concern, so the risk of trying is limited. The cap and mittens combo *Trym* (p. 22) is felted at such a low temperature that shrinking was minimal in my machine; the process just gave the garments a slightly felted and very appealing look.

But the main advantage of small projects is that reward comes quickly, and that it's not the end of the world if they turn out less attractive than you may have hoped for. Small projects are also cool gifts for those who already "have everything"—a handmade bottle holder or a knitted box with a Viking ornament is certainly not something you would find at Sears. In addition, they're great for testing new techniques and new patterns that you may not have seen, or dared to try out, before. In that respect, *The Small Things Matter Collection* is probably my most "beginner friendly" to date.

Well, total beginners may not be the target audience for this book, but a design like the cell phone pouch/glasses case/wrist warmer combo *Asta* (p. 48) could very well serve as a first exercise in lace knitting. All straight pieces, with a sawtooth lace edging, made me classify it as easy. The neckwarmer, however, I've rated as intermediate in terms of skills needed, but it wouldn't be an Elsebeth Lavold collection if there wasn't room for growth as a knitter.

At the other end of the spectrum, there is the shawl *Frida* (p. 17), which is rather complex in terms of the number of charts and schematics needed to describe the design. It's also, in size, a bit on the big side to qualify as a small project. But that's my taste in shawls: I prefer one that's big enough to double as a blanket when for example traveling by train or plane.

On the other hand, Frida is the first ever Viking Knits design with lace ornamentation instead of my usual increases/decreases technique. So here's a chance for those of you who are attracted by the interlace patterns of the Vikings, but not yet comfortable enough with cable knitting to try out the typical Viking Knits designs.

Those of you who do will find several projects in this collection, which is yet another first: I have never before mixed Viking Knits with other types of designs in the same book. Some of them have a medieval flavor, like *Minna* (p. 26), others, like *Monika* (p. 41), are indeed urban in character. But the Viking Knits technique allows for placed motifs, not just full-length cables, and is thus suitable for small projects as well. Those of you who are familiar with my previous Viking Knits books will immediately recognize the pattern elements of *Val* (p. 10), *Trym* (p. 22), and *Borr & Boe* (p. 29), but here they're used in a new ways. The construction of the box Borr, by the way, is inspired by the beautiful bentwood boxes made by Native American tribes of the Pacific Northwest.

So there it is; a mixture of high and low, of small and not-so-small, of party knitting and more demanding projects. Hopefully, there is something to attract both old and new fans of my design work. I've just taught our nine-year-old godson to knit, hint, hint. Happy knitting!

Elsebeth Lavold

Contents

The designs

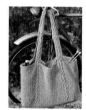

Miscellaneous

Read this before you start

Yarn

The yarn quantities are approximate. They are based on the average requirements of most knitters and apply to the specified yarn. The designer cannot accept responsibility for the result if another yarn is used.

Sizes

Sizes are given from the smallest to the largest, separated by parentheses. If only one number or instruction is given, it applies to all sizes. Lengths are given in inches followed by cm, separated by a slash. All measurements are approximate.

Sizing is made to conform to Crafts Yarn Council standards. See www.yarnstandards.com. Fit is a matter of individual taste and preference. If in doubt, check a favorite sweater and compare to the actual measurements of the garment you want to knit.

Gauge

I strongly recommend that you take the time to knit a swatch and check your gauge before starting a project! This is to ensure that the measurements of your garment will be correct, and to reduce the risk of having to reknit the garment, or parts of it.

Knit a 4 inch / 10 cm square in stockinette stitch, or in pattern if specified in the instructions. If you end up with too many stitches, change to larger needles. If there are too few stitches, change to smaller needles.

If the gauge in stockinette stitch corresponds to the one given, the measurements of your garment will also correspond. Do not measure gauge on a smaller section than 4 inches / 10 cm.

An exact row gauge is only essential when the design is based on whole repeats. If your row gauge differs in such a design, it will affect the length of the garment.

Care

Turn the garment inside out before washing. Check label for washing instructions. Hand wash at low temperature is recommended for most yarns. Always use a mild detergent. Do not soak. For all yarns containing wool, rinse in same temperature. Do not wring; short spin in a washing machine or roll in a towel and press out water. Do not leave wet. Reshape and dry flat, away from heat or direct sunlight. Use a damp pressing cloth when pressing.

Do not store knitted garments hanging.

Do not wash garments unnecessarily, instead air garments often.

Technical information

Please take the time to read the Technical Information on page 60. You will find information about technical details which will make the knitting easier and give your garment a better finish.

We have taken all possible precautions to avoid errors. If you discover an error that has slipped past our pattern check, please let us know at info@ingenkonst.se and we will post a correction at our website www.ingenkonst.se.

elsebeth lavold's

small things matter

val

Medieval times meet the Viking Age in this very contemporary cap-and-gloves combo for young and old. The gloves with the wide cuffs, shown on the next spread, are an accessory Guinevere could very well wear, and I suggest wearing them over a jacket or a heavy sweater to really show them off.

Made with straight cuffs, as here to the right, they're slightly more strict, but still very pretty. The cool cap with the same two intertwined rings and large earflaps completes the design.

Level of Difficulty	Intermediate
Size	Women's
Materials	Silky Wool
Gloves	2 skeins
Cap	2 skeins
Needles	Straight and dpn US size 2 / 3 mm
	Cable needle
Gauge	24 sts × 34 rows in stockinette =
	4 × 4 in / 10 × 10 cm.

Adjust needle size to obtain gauge if necessary.

Welt pattern (worked in the round)
   Rows 1+2: Purl.
   Rows 3+4: Knit.
Repeat these 4 rows.

Welt pattern (worked back and forth)
   Row 1 (WS): Knit.
   Rows 2+3: Purl.
   Row 4: Knit.
Repeat these 4 rows.

Gloves, right glove

Cast on 42 sts; divide onto dpn and join to work in the round, being careful not to twist cast-on row. Work in stockinette for 2½ in / 6 cm. Mark placement of thumb by working *the first 8 sts* with contrast color waste yarn. Move the sts back to left needle and then continue in stockinette for another 2½ in / 6 cm (the glove now measures 5 in / 12 cm total). Place the first 16 sts on a holder = palm and the last 16 sts on another holder = back of hand.

Little finger: Divide the remaining 10 sts onto 3 dpn. Cast on 2 new sts between the little and ring fingers = 12 sts and work around in stockinette for 2 in / 5 cm (= middle of little finger nail). K2tog around and then knit 1 round; cut yarn and pull tail through remaining sts. Divide the 32 sts from holders onto dpn and pick up and knit 2 new sts at base of little finger = 34 sts. Knit 4 rounds.

Ring finger: Knit 5 sts from palm, the 2 st at base of little finger, knit 5 sts from back of hand and cast on 2 new sts at base of middle finger. Divide these 14 sts

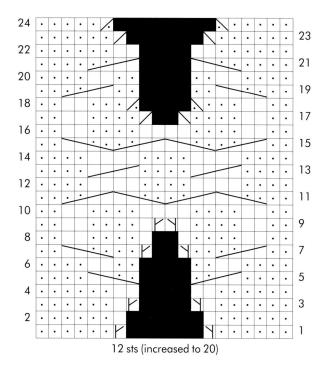

12 sts (increased to 20)

onto 3 dpn and knit around for 2¾ in / 7 cm or to middle of ring finger nail. Shape top and finish as for little finger.

Middle finger: Work as for ring finger, adding 2 sts each at base of ring and index fingers, and shaping top when finger measures 3¼ in / 8 cm.

Index finger: Knit the remaining 12 sts and pick up and knit 2 new sts at the base of middle finger. Divide these 14 sts onto 3 dpn work as for ring finger.

Thumb: Remove contrast color yarn and divide the sts onto 3 dpn; pick up and knit 2 sts at each side between the upper and lower sides of thumbhole = 19 sts (8 sts on bottom of thumbhole, 7 at top + 2 at each side). Knit around in stockinette for 2¼ in / 5½ cm or to middle of thumbnail. Shape as for fingers.

Left glove

Work as for right glove, reversing shaping. Mark placement for thumb by working *the last 8 sts* with contrast color yarn.

Straight cuff

Pick up and knit 40 sts, beginning at outer side of glove and work around in welt pattern, increasing 4 sts evenly spaced around on 1st round = 44 sts. After working 3 pattern repeats, place markers around the 12 sts at center of back of hand and work charted motif over these 12 sts. After completing charted rows, continue in welt pattern until there are 4 pattern repeats following the motif. Bind off in knitting.

Gauntlet cuff

Pick up and knit 40 sts, beginning at outer side of glove and work around in welt pattern. Place markers at each side of glove and increase 1 st at each side of markers on every 8th round throughout. After completing 3 pattern repeats, place markers around the 12 sts at center of back of hand and work charted motif over these 12 sts. After completing charted rows, continue in welt pattern until there are 5 pattern repeats following the motif. Bind off in knitting.

Cap

Cast on 110 sts and work back and forth in welt pattern; the 1st row = WS. After working 9 rows, work charted motif over the 12 center sts. After completing charted rows, work another 10 rows in welt pattern. On the next row 1 of pattern, place markers to divide cap into 5 sections of 22 sts each. Shape crown as follows: * K2tog, knit to 2 sts before next marker, ssk; repeat from * across row. Repeat this decrease row on every 4th row until 12 sts remain in each section. Now decrease on both rows 1 and 4 until 2 sts remain in each section = 10 sts total. Cut yarn, leaving a tail of 11¾ in / 30 cm, and pull tail through remaining sts. Use remaining tail to seam cap after finishing.

Ear flaps (work both alike): Pick up and knit 20 sts on lower edge of cap, 2 in / 5 cm from side, and work in welt pattern, beginning on row 3 (=WS). Now work 6 pattern repeats. On the next row 1 of pattern, begin shaping: * K2tog, knit until 2 sts remain, ssk.

Decrease the same way on every 4th row a total of 3 times. Bind off.

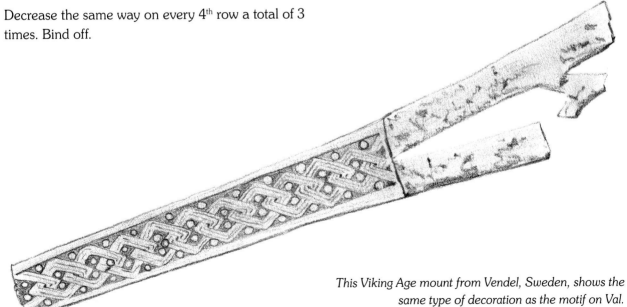

This Viking Age mount from Vendel, Sweden, shows the same type of decoration as the motif on Val.

sol

Wool and silk are just superior fibers for socks, so I thought I should include a pair. *Helena Norén,* the sample garment knitter who has been with me the longest, lives close to the Polar Circle, and that has made her a skilled sock knitter. Not being one myself, I asked her to make a pair of socks using this small Viking cable on the outside of the shin.

They turned out very pretty, and now that we present them, she should have part of the credit. Sol, by the way, is the Swedish word for Sun, so they'll hopefully bring sunny days to your feet.

Level of Difficulty	Intermediate
Sizes	Women's (Men's)
Materials	Silky Wool 2 skeins
Needles	US size 2 / 3 mm
	Dpn US size 2 / 3 mm
	Cable needle
Gauge	24 sts in stockinette = 4 in / 10 cm.
	28 sts in cable panel = 3¼ in / 8 cm.

Adjust needle size to obtain gauge if necessary.
Ribbing K2, p2. Make sure that you have 2 knit sts at outer edge of each RS row.

Right sock

Leg: Cast on 56 (64) sts and work back and forth. Set up pattern, the 1st row = WS: *P2, k2; repeat from * 5 (6) times, 16 sts following chart, * p2, k2; repeat from * 5 (6) times. Continue in pattern, with 20 (24) sts in ribbing at each side and the center 16 sts in charted pattern. First work rows 0–6, and then repeat rows 7–14 6 (7) times. End with rows 15–20. The leg should now be 6¾ (8) in / 17 (20) cm long and there should be 52 (60) sts remaining.

Divide the sts onto 4 dpn (13 (15) sts on each needle); mark the beginning of the round and work around in stockinette for 5 rounds.

Heel: Work back and forth in stockinette over sts on needles 1 and 2 for 18 (24) rows. Foot measurements are taken from this point! *Now work short rows:* Work 15 (19) sts, ssk; turn and work 5 sts, k2tog; turn and work 6 sts, ssk; turn and work 7 sts, k2tog, etc., until no more decreases can be made. Slip the first st after each turn. The last row has 14 (18) sts.

Now work around all sts on dpn: work 14 (18) sts of heel, pick up and knit 18 (22) sts along heel flap, work sts on needles 3 and 4 in stockinette and pick up and knit 18 (22) sts on other side of heel flap. There should now be 76 (84) sts around. Move the marker for beginning of round back to its original place.

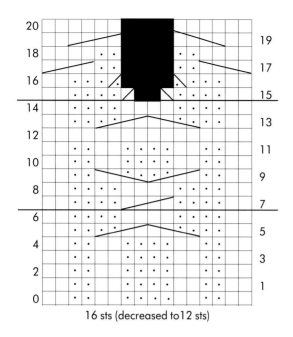

16 sts (decreased to 12 sts)

Make a gusset on each side of heel: On needle 1, ssk, k23 (25); on needle 2, k23 (25), k2tog; work sts on needles 3 and 4 in stockinette. Decrease the same way on every row until there are 13 (15) sts on each needle. Work in stockinette until foot measures 8 (9) in / 20 (23) cm or desired length.

Toe: Needle 1: K1, ssk, k10 (12); needle 2: K10 (12), k2tog, k1; needle 3: as for needle 1, and work needle 4 as for needle 2. Decrease as set on every row until 8 sts remain. Cut yarn and pull though remaining sts; tighten and weave in tail neatly on WS. Seam leg using a full st as seam allowance.

Left sock

Work as for right sock but reverse shaping—the heel is worked on needles 3 and 4.

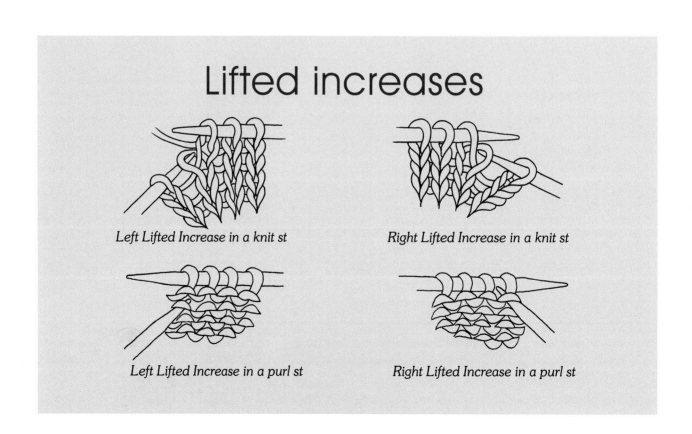

Lifted increases

Left Lifted Increase in a knit st

Right Lifted Increase in a knit st

Left Lifted Increase in a purl st

Right Lifted Increase in a purl st

frida

Roll out the red carpet for a world premiere: Viking Knits have conquered lace! In this lovely shawl, the Twined Cable, the Four-knot and the Ring give the garment an unmistakable Viking flavor, but in a different technique. The generous size makes it a perfect wrap for summer evenings, or for an evening out.

I've rated it as Intermediate, and keeping track of all these pattern elements craves some attention, so we've photographed the shawl from several different angles, and included a schematic of the overall design.

Level of Difficulty	Intermediate
Size	26 × 76 in / 66 × 192 cm
Materials	7 skeins Silky Wool
Needles	US size 7 / 4½ mm
Gauge	20 sts × 28 rows in stockinette = 4 × 4 in / 10 × 10 cm.

Adjust needle size to obtain gauge if necessary.

Note On the charts, all even-numbered rows are purled except for the 5 garter sts at each side.

Chart 1 shows the sections of the repeat where the corners meet the vertical repeats which are then automatically placed correctly on the piece.

Cast on 131 sts and knit 9 rows; the 1st row = WS. Work in stockinette and pattern, except for the outer 5 sts at each side which are worked in garter st throughout. Work the first 4 rows in stockinette. Now place the edge panel using chart 1: 5 garter sts, Corner A, 8 sts of X-repeat 11 times (88 sts), Corner B, and then 5 garter sts.

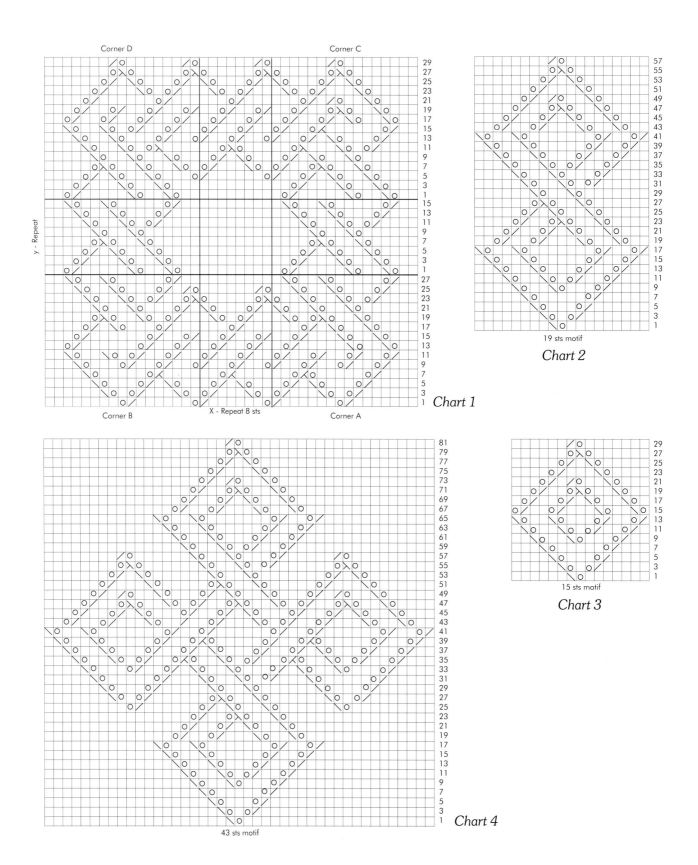

Corner D   Corner C

29
27
25
23
21
19
17
15
13
11
9
7
5
3
1

y - Repeat

15
13
11
9
7
5
3
1

27
25
23
21
19
17
15
13
11
9
7
5
3
1

X - Repeat 8 sts

Corner B   Corner A

Chart 1

57
55
53
51
49
47
45
43
41
39
37
35
33
31
29
27
25
23
21
19
17
15
13
11
9
7
5
3
1

19 sts motif

Chart 2

81
79
77
75
73
71
69
67
65
63
61
59
57
55
53
51
49
47
45
43
41
39
37
35
33
31
29
27
25
23
21
19
17
15
13
11
9
7
5
3
1

43 sts motif

Chart 4

29
27
25
23
21
19
17
15
13
11
9
7
5
3
1

15 sts motif

Chart 3

18

At the end of row 28, the lower edge panel is complete and then you can begin the edge panels following the Y-repeat (16 rows).

At the same time, work 4 rows in stockinette between the edge panels before starting on the motifs.

** Work the motif following chart 2 inside 25 sts at each side (4 sts inside the edge panel).

At the same time, when beginning row 15 on chart 2, begin working motif on chart 3 at the center of the shawl.

After completing chart 2, work 2 rows in stockinette.*

Now work motif on chart 4 centered on shawl.

At the same time as working row 27 on chart 4, begin working motif on chart 3 directly above the motif from chart 2—it should be 27 sts in from each side—6 sts in from the edge panel.

After completing motif on chart 4, work 2 rows in stockinette.

Repeat from ** 2 times and then work ** – * so that the shawl patterns are balanced.

Work 2 rows in stockinette between the edge panels.

Now the last Y-repeat should be complete (30 repeats).

Work the final edge panel: 5 garter sts, Corner C, 8 sts X-repeat 11 times (88 sts), Corner D, and 5 garter sts.

At the end of row 30, the top panel is complete.

Work 2 rows in stockinette between the garter borders.

Knit 10 rows in garter st and then bind off.

Finishing

Block shawl.

The four-knot is used on many Viking Age objects, among them this golden brooch from Hedeby, originally a Danish settlement, but today on the German side of the border. Recreated in lace knitting on Frida *and in the traditional Viking Knits technique on* Borr & Boe *(page 29).*

trym

The magnificent runestone we used as backdrop is placed outside the church of Danderyd, north of Stockholm, but that's not where it stood originally. It may seem strange to move a runestone right next to a church wall, but as you can see in the photo on the next spread, the cross indicates that the stone was erected after Christianity came to the area, so I guess the move was approved by the 14th century priests.

Viking Age ornaments are always distinctive and decorative. Here I have used a Ring and Cross motif on both the cap and the mittens. The whole set is then lightly felted for added warmth.

Level of Difficulty   Intermediate

Sizes

Mittens child's 8–10 years (woman's)

Cap   child's small (child's large) woman's (man's)

Materials Silky Wool

Mittens 1 skein

Cap   2 skeins

Needles   US size 6 / 4 mm

Cable needle

Gauge   22 sts in pattern = 4 in / 10 cm.

Adjust needle size to obtain gauge if necessary.

Note Worked without edge stitches; the first and last sts of the pattern are used for seaming.

Pattern

Row 1: Knit.

Row 2: Purl.

Row 3: * K2, p2; repeat from * and end with k2.

Row4: * P2, k2; repeat from * and end with p2.

Repeat these 4 rows.

Cap

Brim: Cast on 98 (106) 114 (122) sts and knit 1 row, purl 1 row, knit 1 row for the edging. *Next row, RS:* Work pattern rows 1–4 and then rows 1+2. *Place motifs:* Work 14 (18) 18 (22) sts in pattern, 14 sts from chart, * 14 (14) 18 (18) sts in pattern, 14 sts from chart, repeat from * 1 time and end with 14 (18) 18 (22) sts in pattern. After completing charted rows, work rows 1–4 and then rows 1+2 in pattern.

Work edging for fold: Work (purl 1 row, knit 1 row) 3 times = 6 rows in reverse stockinette. Now work in stockinette for about 4 in / 10 cm (the smooth/knit side will be against the head, that is, on what is now the WS of work).

Crown: Now work stockinette on the RS, that is, the side that has been reverse stockinette up until now. Increase 0 (4) 8 (0) sts evenly spaced over the first row = 98 (110) 122 (122) sts. Place markers to divide the piece into 6 sections of 16 (18) 20 (20) sts + a seam stitch at beginning and end of row. *Decrease row:* K1,

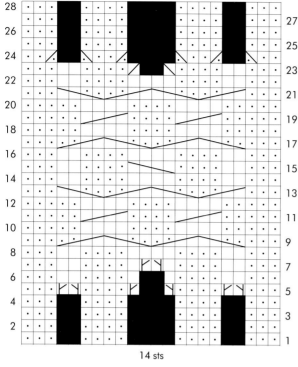

Chart for the cap

14 sts

ssk, knit to 2 sts before marker, k2tog; repeat * – * on each section and end with k1. Decrease the same way on, alternately, every other and every 4th row until 12 sts remain. Cut yarn (leaving a tail of about 9¾ in / 25 cm) and pull tail through remaining sts.

Mittens

Left mitten Cast on 34 (42) sts and knit 1 row, purl 1 row, knit 1 row for the edging. *Next row, RS:* Begin working in pattern. After 2 repeats, work rows 1 and 2 and then, on the next RS row, begin *thumb gusset:* Work 17 (21) sts, LLI, RLI and then complete row. Work 3 rows in pattern, keeping the new sts for the

thumb gusset in stockinette. *Next row:* Work 17 (21) sts, LLI, k2, RLI and complete row. Work 3 rows. Continue increasing the same way at each side within the 17 (21) sts on every 4th row (there are 2 more sts between increases each time) until thumb gusset has 14 (18) sts. *At the same time,* after 4 (6) pattern repeats, work rows 1 and 2 and then work charted motif. Place the motif between the sts for the thumb gusset and the *last* 2 sts on the row. Do not cut yarn. *Thumb:* Using a new strand of yarn, work 8 (12) rows in stockinette over the 14 (18) sts for thumb. K2tog across and then cut yarn and pull tail through remaining sts. *Hand:* Continue as set, picking up and knitting 2 new sts over thumbhole (in the 2 outermost sts of thumb). After completing charted motif, end by repeating the pattern 3 (4) times. *Shape top* on RS rows: K1, * ssk, work to 2 sts before the center, k2tog *; repeat * – * and end with k1. Repeat the decreases on every other row until 14 (22) sts remain. Work 1 WS row. Work to center of mitten; place the two halves with right sides facing and knit together using 1 st from each needle; bind off at the same time (= three-needle bind-off).

Right mitten Work as for left mitten, but the motif is placed between the *first* 2 sts and the thumb gusset.

Finishing

Mittens: Sew thumb and side seams, grafting within the seam stitches.
Cap: Seam cap by grafting inside the seam stitches, on the pattern side of the brim, on the smooth side of the crown, and on the reverse stockinette side in between.
Seam at center back and crown.

If you like a slightly felted look, the Trym design is well suited for felting. You can read more about felting Silky Wool garments on page 40.

Chart for the mittens

children 14 sts
women 18 sts

The sweater our pretty model is wearing in the photos is Hekla from The Second Viking Knits Collection

minna

Medieval influences remain strong in my designs. This set is in part inspired by medieval helmets and hoods, but it's something of a chameleon—the character changes dramatically with how you combine it.

Wear it "fully exposed", as in this photo, and you can walk right into one of the medieval festivals that are presently very popular in Sweden. Wear it with a fitted coat or a leather jacket, as in the photo on the next spread, and you've taken a giant step into the 21st century.

Level of Difficulty	Intermediate
Sizes	Child's (Woman's) Man's
Materials	Silky Wool
Full set	3 skeins
Cap	1 skein
Wrist Warmers	1 skein
Neck Warmer	2 skeins
Needles	16-, 24-, 32-inch / 40, 60 and 80 cm circulars US size 6 / 4 mm
	Dpn US size 6 / 4 mm
Gauge	22 sts × 30 rows = 4 × 4 in / 10 × 10 cm.

Adjust needle size to obtain gauge if necessary.

4-stitch Cable
  Rows 1+2+3: K4.
  Row 4: 2/2 right cable (see page 63).
Repeat these 4 rows.

Cap
With shortest circular, cast on 116 (124) 132 sts; join, being careful not to twist cast-on row. Set up pattern:

* Work 25 (27) 29 sts in ribbing as follows: (p1, k1) 12 (13) 14 times, p1, 4-st cable; repeat from * 3 times. Work in pattern for 3½ (4¼) 5¼ in / 9 (11) 13 cm. Next, decrease as follows: * p1, k3tog, work until 4 sts before cable, sk2p, p1, 4-st cable; repeat from * 3 times. Decrease the same way on every 4th row as long as possible. There should now be 9 (11) 9 sts in each section and 36 (44) 36 sts across row. On the next row, knit the center 2 sts of cable together = 32 (40) 32 sts. On the next row, sk2p over the 3 cable sts and s2kp2 over the center 3 rib sts in each section. Cut yarn and pull through remaining sts. Weave in tail neatly on WS.

Neckwarmer (worked from the top down)
With short circular, cast on 84 (92) 100 sts; join, being careful not to twist cast-on row. Set up pattern:
* Work 17 (19) 21 sts in ribbing as follows: (p1, k1) 8 (9) 10 times, p1, 4-st cable; repeat from * 3 times. Work in pattern for 3¼ (3½) 3½ in / 8 (9) 9 cm or desired length. If you want just a simple neckwarmer, bind off at this point. If you want to protect your shoul-

ders also, continue as follows: * P1, k1, p1, work (k1, p1, k1) in the same st (= 2 sts added), work until 4 sts before cable, (k1, p1, k1) in the same st (2 sts added), P1, k1, p1 and then work 4-st cable; repeat from * 3 times. Increase the same way on every 4th row until piece measures 6 in / 15 cm from the 1st increase. Bind off in pattern.

Wrist Warmers

With dpn, cast on 37 (41) 45 sts, dividing sts evenly between 4 dpn; join to work in the round. Work 17 (19) 21 sts in ribbing as follows: (p1, k1) 8 (9) 10 times, p1, 4-st cable, 16 (18) 20 sts in ribbing: (p1, k1) 8 (9) 10 times. Work in pattern for 1½ (2) 2½ in / 4 (5) 6 cm. *Thumb gusset:* work until 10 sts before cable (the last st should be a purl), LLI, k1, RLI, complete round. After each increase round, there will be 2 more sts between increases; work all added sts in stockinette. Increase the same way on every other round 2 times and then on every 4th round until there are 11 (13) 15 sts for thumb gusset. When gusset measures 2 (2¾) 3½ in / 5 (7) 9 cm from 1st increase, bind off all gusset sts. Cast on 1 st at back of thumb and continue in pattern as before for another ¾ (1¼) 1½ in / 2 (3) 4 cm. Bind off all sts in pattern. Work the other wrist warmer the same way, reversing placement of thumb gusset (the thumb gusset should be placed the same number of sts after the cable).

borr & boe

It started with a cell phone pouch. With a few extra stitches, it becomes a passport pouch. Knit it with the yarn held double, add a bottom and a shoulder strap, felt it slightly, and you have a perfect water bottle carrier. Omit the strap: A wine cooler.

Then I made versions with four sides, in single and double yarn, to create cool containers for all the little things we surround ourselves with—pencils, make-up, rechargeable batteries... Or it could be a flower pot. Whichever container you make, I'm sure you'll find a use for it. All items are decorated with a four-knot.

Borr Bottleholder & box

Level of Difficulty Fairly easy

Sizes

Bottleholder will fit a 50 (100) cl bottle

Small box 4 × 4 × 4¾ in / 10 × 10 × 12 cm

Large box 5½ × 5½ × 6 in / 14 × 14 × 15 cm

Materials Silky Wool 1 skein per project

For box: Wood glue, plastic bag, form for drying box

Needles US size 8 / 5 mm

2 dpn US size 8 / 5 mm

Cable needle

Gauge 16 sts × 24 rows in stockinette with yarn held double = 4 × 4 in / 10 × 10 cm.

Adjust needle size to obtain gauge if necessary.

Bottleholder

With yarn held double, cast on 38 (46) sts and work as follows (the 1st row = WS): * P2, k16 (20), repeat from * and end with p2. Next row (RS): Knit. The pattern features 16 (20) sts in garter st between 2 knit ribs with

2 sts each. Repeat these 2 rows 3 times (= a total of 6 rows). Now work reverse stockinette between the knit ribs. When piece is 1½ (2) in / 4 (5) cm long, work a knot motif at center of each reverse stockinette section. After completing knot motif, work reverse stockinette between knit ribs. When piece measures 8 (9½) in / 20 (24) cm, knit bottom in garter st. On the first row of the bottom, decrease to eliminate the edge st at each side. On larger size, also decrease the 2 center sts on each half to 1 st = 36 (42) sts. On the next row, divide piece into 6 sections of 6 (7) sts each, placing a marker between each section. Next RS row: * Work until 2 sts before marker, k2tog, repeat from * across row = 6 sts decreased. Repeat decrease row on every other row until 12 sts remain. Cut yarn, leaving a 12 in / 30 cm tail. Pull tail through remaining sts and then seam bottleholder.

Finishing

Seam holder—graft from knot to knot in garter stitch and then through 1 knit st at each side. With dpn, cast on 4 sts and knit an I-cord (see page 57) about

23½ in / 60 cm long or desired length. Securely attach I-cord above the center knit ribs. Knit another I-cord about 2½ in / 6 cm long and sew it as a loop above seamline. Lightly felt holder in washer (about 100F / 40C—read more about felting on page 40). Shape holder around a suitable bottle and let dry.

Box

For the smaller box work with one strand of yarn, for the larger work with two strands.

Cast on 90 sts with and work as follows (the 1st row = WS): * P2, k20, repeat from * 3 times and end with p2. Next row (RS): Knit. The pattern features 20 sts in garter st between 2 knit ribs with 2 sts each. Repeat these 2 rows 3 times. Now work reverse stockinette between the knit ribs. When piece is ¾ (1½) in / 2 (4) cm long, work a knot motif at the center of each reverse stockinette section. After completing knot motif, work reverse stockinette between knit ribs. When piece measures 4¾ (6) in / 12 (15) cm, bind off the outermost st at each side and place a marker at the center of each

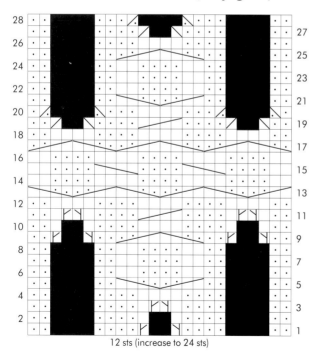

12 sts (increase to 24 sts)

knit rib. Work in garter st and decrease as follows on every RS row: * K2tog, work until 2 sts before marker, ssk. Repeat from * across row. Decrease the same way on every RS row until 8 sts remain. Cut yarn, leaving a 12 in / 30 cm tail. Pull tail through remaining sts and then use it to seam box.

Finishing

Seam box—graft from knot to knot in garter stitch and then with 1 knit st as seam allowance at sides. Dampen box and then press out as much water as possible. Dip box into wood glue and let glue soak in. Squeeze out glue and then shape box over a suitable form. You can use a paper carton or plastic box or you can make a form by taping together cardstock paper in the appropriate size. Cover with a plastic bag so that the box won't get glued to the form. Let dry completely.

Boe Phone pouch (Passport pouch)

Level of Difficulty   Fairly easy
Size   3¼ × 4¼ (4 × 7) in
            8 × 11 (10 × 18) cm
Materials   Silky Wool 1 skein
            1 rather large decorative button
                for passport pouch
Needles   US size 6 / 4 mm
            2 dpn US size 6 / 4 mm
            Cable needle
Gauge   22 sts × 30 rows in stockinette =
            4 × 4 in / 10 × 10 cm.
Adjust needle size to obtain gauge if necessary.

Cast on 20 (24) sts and work as follows (the 1st row = WS): P2, k16 (20), p2. *Next row, RS:* Knit. The pattern features 16 (20) sts in garter st between 2 knit ribs with 2 sts each. Repeat these 2 rows 3 (4) times (= a total of 6 (8) rows). Now work in reverse stockinette between the knit ribs. When piece is 4¼ (7) in / 11 (18) cm long, place a marker at each side. Work as

set for ⅜ (1¼) in / 1 (3) cm and then work knot motif at center. After completing charted motif, continue with reverse stockinette between the knit ribs and then, at the same lenght as back, finish the pouch with edging as at beginning. On the passport pouch, make a buttonhole as follows: on the 5th row of edging, k10, bind off 4 sts, k10. On the next row, cast on 4 new sts over bound-off sts and continue until edging rows are complete. Bind off in knitting on RS.

Finishing

Fold pouch at markers and sew sides by grafting into outermost sts. With dpn, cast on 4 sts and knit an I-cord (see p. 57) about 23½ in / 60 cm long or desired length. Securely attach I-cord at each side above the knit ribs. Sew button onto passport pouch.

The sweater our pretty model is wearing in the photo is Runnel from The Out of the Woods Collection.

brita

All the major Haute Couture shows end with a bride's outfit, so I put mine in the middle. I may someday design a bride's gown, but for the small projects book, I settled for a scarf and elegant half-gloves.

The half-gloves will complement many styles of bridal dresses and add both warmth and romance. Match it with a shawl to cover the shoulders and to make the bride even prettier. If marriage is not where you're at, the pillow will still look adorable, and supply a touch of romance to any room.

Level of Difficulty   Intermediate

Sizes

Shawl   19¾ × 55 in / 50 × 140 cm

Sleeves Women's smaller (larger)
Arm circumference up to 10¾ (13) in / 27 (33) cm
Length 11 in / 28 cm along seam line

Materials Silky Wool 6 skeins
(5 for the shawl, 1 for sleeves)

Needles US sizes 4, 6, and 7 / 3.5, 4, and 4.5 mm
Crochet hook US size F / 6 mm

Gauge 22 sts × 30 rows in stockinette on US 6 / 4 mm = 4 × 4 in / 10 × 10 cm.
20 sts × 28 rows in stockinette on US 7 / 4.5 mm = 4 × 4 in / 10 × 10 cm.

Adjust needle sizes to obtain gauge if necessary.

Edge Stitches The outermost st at each side is worked in stockinette, except on garter edges.

Shawl

With US 6 / 4 mm needles, cast on 101 sts and work in garter st; the 1st row = WS. Decrease 1 st at each side on every RS row 2 times = 97 sts. After completing 5th row (3 garter ridges on RS), change to US 7 / 4.5 mm needles and stockinette. Work 2 rows and then work in pattern following chart 1, rows 1–24. Now repeat rows 25–44 until shawl is about 25½ in / 65 cm long (ending with row 44 of the chart). Bind off leaving a long tail. Make another piece the same way but a half repeat longer (end after row 33 in pattern).

Finishing

Graft the two pieces—unpick the bound-off sts on each piece and graft the live sts as invisibly as possible. With US 6 / 4 mm needles (a circular is recommended), pick up and knit sts along one long side of shawl. Pick up and knit 2 sts for every 3 rows inside a ½ st. Work in garter st, increasing 1 st at the beginning of every row 4 times (2 sts increased at each side). When there are 3 garter ridges on RS, bind off in knitting on RS. Invisibly graft the corner and crochet a picot edging all around the shawl: * 2 sc, ch 4, insert hook into first chain and work 1 sc. Repeat from *. Block shawl.

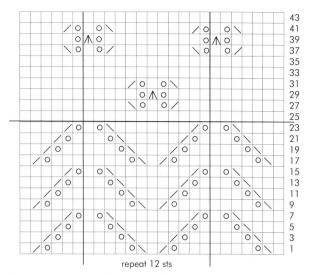

Chart 1 shows only RS rows. All WS rows are purled across.

Sleeves

With needles US 6 / 4 mm, cast on 39 (43) sts and work in garter st; the 1st row = WS. Make a double decrease (S2Kp2) at the center of *every* RS row 2 times = 35 (39) sts. Shape point at lower edge: Mark off the 3 center sts. Work to first marker and then work short rows following chart 2. After completing all short rows, work across rest of row and then back across entire row. All measurements are taken from this point! Now work in flower pattern following chart 1, first working rows 39–44, and then repeating rows 25–44. After 1¼ in / 3 cm, begin increasing 1 st at each side (inside the outermost st at each side) on every 6th row 7 times = 49 (53) sts. Work new sts in pattern as soon as there are enough for a complete flower. When piece measures 4¾–5½ in / 12–14 cm (ending on a complete or half repeat), work wave pattern following chart rows 1–24 (make sure that the pattern is correctly placed in relation to the flowers). When wave pattern is complete, work 2 rows in stockinette. Change to US 4 / 3.5 mm needles and work 6 rows in garter st. Bind off in knitting on RS.

Finishing

Crochet a picot edging around the top and bottom edges. Graft seam using ½ st as seam allowance.

Brita Pillow

Level of Difficulty	Intermediate
Measurements	16 × 16 in / 40 × 40 cm
Materials	Silky Wool 2 skeins.
	Fabric for backing, about 18 × 18 in / 45 × 45 cm and pillow form to fit
Needles	16-, 24-, and 32-inch / 40, 60, and 80 cm circulars US size 4 / 3.5 mm
	Dpn US size 4 / 3.5 mm
	Crochet hook US size F / 6 mm
Gauge	24 sts × 34 rows in stockinette = 4 × 4 in / 10 × 10 cm.

Adjust needle size to obtain gauge if necessary.

Note The pillow is knit in the round from the outer edge in towards the center.

Front

Cast on 376 sts and join, being careful not to twist cast-on row. Work around in stockinette. Mark 1st st at beginning of round and 1 st at each corner (= 93 sts for each side of the pillow + 4 corner sts).

Knit 2 rounds in stockinette without any decreases. On the next round, set up pattern and begin shaping:

* Knit one st which will be the corner st, k2tog, k2 and then begin charted pattern. Begin at the 1st st and work across to beginning of pattern repeat, work repeat 6 times, and end with remaining sts of charted row, k2, ssk. Repeat from * on each of the pillow's 4 sides.

Decrease in this manner on each side of the corner sts. Work decreases on 2 rounds one after the other (that is, on a pattern round and then on a plain round) and then work 1 round without any decreases (rounds without any decreases alternate between pattern and plain rounds). After eliminating all the stockinette sts, work pattern out to the sides. Each yarnover is paired with a decrease. If you can't work both, work those sts in stockinette. Make sure that the pattern doesn't get out of alignment. After completing round 24, continue, repeating rounds 25–44 throughout. *At the same time, decrease as before. If you don't have room for a com-*

plete flower, work in stockinette instead. When 8 sts remain, cut yarn and pull through remaining sts.

Finishing

Block piece. Crochet a picot edging as for shawl around all the edges. For back of pillow, cut out fabric somewhat larger than size of knit and blocked front. Measure and steam press down seam allowance around all four sides of fabric. Sew fabric to knit front around 3 sides; insert pillow form and seam last side. A pillow form in a contrasting color will look nice.

Chart 2

hedda

In *The Dreamweaver Collection,* we included Anders' motorcycle in one of the photos. This time, we chose his other two-wheeler; not nearly as well polished, and, to be frank about it, not nearly as much used either. But the photo came out nice.

So did Hedda. I love the way a simple block pattern sets off a cable that extends into the handles. Here I've used the pattern elements for a large tote that's just lightly felted. A sturdy lining is a must, but then you have a tote that is both very attractive and highly versatile.

Level of Difficulty   Intermediate

Size   Bottom 17¼ × 4¾ in / 44 × 12 cm

Height 12¼ in / 31 cm before felting

(Felting, see page 40)

Materials   Silky Wool 6–7 skeins

Fabric for lining etc., see finishing below

Needles   US size 10 / 6 mm

24-inch / 60 cm circular US size 10 / 6 mm

Cable needle

Gauge   15 sts × 22 rows in stockinette with yarn held double = 4 × 4 in / 10 × 10 cm.

Adjust needle size to obtain gauge if necessary.

Note The bag is knit with yarn held double. Do not splice in both strands at the same place.

Handles (make 4)

With yarn held double, cast on 12 sts and work back and forth following chart. Repeat rows 1–12 for 8 in / 20 cm ending with row 12. Set piece aside.

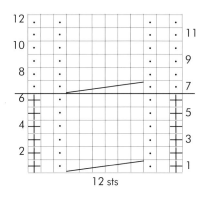

12 sts

Bag body

* Work the 12 sts of first handle, but work these 12 sts following chart rows 13–24; knit cast-on 30 sts; work the 12 sts of second handle as for the first, and then knit cast-on 42 sts; repeat from * = 192 sts. Now work pattern in the round as follows: ** begin with 12 sts of first handle, (k6, p6) 2 times, k6, 12 sts of second handle, (k6, p6) 3 times, k6; repeat from **.

The pattern is set up so that there is a knit block on each side of each handle. Continue in pattern as set until the block is 12 rows high. Change sequence so that you have a knit block over a reverse stockinette block and vice versa. Make this set of blocks 12 rows high. Continue, alternating stockinette and reverse stockinette blocks until there are 6 blocks in length and the bag measures 11¾ in / 30 cm.

Knit 1 row, decreasing 2 sts in each cable (8 sts decreased across row) = 184 sts. Purl 3 rows. Place a marker 2 blocks out from each handle on the section with 7 blocks. The 3 blocks between the markers will be the sides of the bag.

Now work the bottom in stockinette: work until 2 sts before 1st marker, ssk, slm, k2tog; repeat the decreases at each marker and then finish row. Work 1 row without any decreases. Continue, alternating decrease and plain rows until there are no more sts on the short sides. Divide sts onto two needles and bind off using a three-needle bind-off.

Finishing

Work a row of single crochet around all the edges. Felt bag (see below).

Line bag with heavy fabric. Cut lining to measurements of felted bag + seam allowances. It is better for the lining to be too big rather than too small. Seam lining along sides and bottom, mitering corners. If desired, cut a piece of foam padding to shape the bottom of the bag. Insert foam and then sew lining into bag.

Felting

Turn the piece(s) inside out, place in a pillow case and wash with similar color clothes in a full load of wash. It is important that you wash with a full load so they won't felt too much. Use a detergent without bleach!

If you want a light felting with only marginal shrinkage, use cool cycle, (water temperature about 104 F / 40 C).

If you use the warm cycle (140 F / 60 C), there will be some shrinkage. How much depends on your machine and the size of your load. My pieces shrank around 10%.

Shape and let dry.

For a bag, the exact size isn't important, so the amount of shrinkage is of no consequence.

monika

I get the impression that many people seem to think that you can't look *elegant* in knitwear. I'm pretty sure that those who claim such views can't be knitters themselves. I can't say that I designed Monika specifically to prove them wrong, but when I look at the photos, I get a warm feeling of having made a point in the debate.

The welt pattern is one of my favorites. I keep coming back to versions of it. Here I have combined it with short-row shaping to give both the hat and the bag a chic and urban feel. I've used six colors, but it would also look great in two or three.

Level of Difficulty		Easy
Sizes	*Cap*	Women's
	Bag	8¾ × 7½ in / 22 × 19 cm
Materials		Silky Wool (for both pieces)
		1 skein main color (MC)
		1 skein each of 5 contrast colors (CC)

The colors used in the samples are:

MC	071 Flourite Blue
CC1	046 Midnight Blue
CC2	058 Columbine
CC3	057 Old Lilac
CC4	005 Lava
CC5	063 Purple

Needles	US sizes 6 and 7 / 4 and 4.5 mm
	2 dpn US size 6 / 4 mm
	(*Optional:* handles, see Finishing)
Gauge	18 sts × 36 rows in garter st on larger
	needles with yarn held double =
	4 × 4 in / 10 × 10 cm.

Adjust needle sizes to obtain gauge if necessary.
Note Edge sts are worked in stockinette.

Welt pattern

Row 1 with CC: Knit.
Row 2 with CC: Knit.
Rows 3+5 with CC: Purl.
Rows 4+6 with CC: Knit.
Row 7 with MC: Knit.
Row 8 with MC: Purl.

Repeat these 8 rows.

On each row 1 and 3 catch the contrast color tails as you knit so that you won't have to weave in so many tails afterwards (see page 47). Carry MC up along side throughout.

Bag

With larger needles and CC1 (Midnight Blue) yarn held double, cast on 60 sts and knit 1 row, purl 1 row, knit 1 row. Now work welt pattern, beginning on row 3. Work the pattern in the following color sequence: Midnight Blue, Columbine, Old Lilac, Lava, Purple, Lava, Old Lilac, Columbine, Midnight Blue and then purl 1 row, knit 1 row with the last color. Bind off.

Cap

With larger needles and CC1 (Midnight Blue) yarn held double, cast on 96 sts and knit 1 row, purl 1 row, knit 1 row. Now work welt pattern, beginning on row 3. Instead of rows 7 and 8, work short rows with MC as follows: k78; turn and p58; turn and k78; turn and p98. Work 1 repeat with CC1 (Midnight Blue), 1 with CC2 (Columbine), 1 with CC3 (Old Lilac), 1 with CC4 (Lava), 1 CC5 (Purple), 1 with CC4 (Lava), and 1 with CC3 (Old Lilac) and then purl 1 row, knit 1 row with the last color. Knit the crown with MC: cast on an edge st on each side and work in stockinette for rest of cap. After row 2 mark off 6 sections with 16 sts each. Decrease row: edge st, * ssk, work until 2 sts before marker, k2tog; repeat from * across row and end with edge st. Decrease in this manner on every other row. When 14 sts remain (6 groups of 2 sts each), work edge st, * k2tog; repeat from * and end with edge st. Cut yarn and pull through remaining sts; weave in tail neatly on WS.

Finishing

Cap Seam cap by grafting as invisibly as possible, sewing only into contrast color rows so that the colors align at seam. Pull seam together slightly. Graft crown inside the edge sts.

With smaller needles and your choice of CC yarn held double, cast on 17 sts and knit 9 rows garter st. Bind off in knitting. Pin strip vertically to cap to hide the seam and attach short ends at the top and bottom (see photo).

Bag Upper edge With smaller needles and your choice of CC held double, pick up and knit 29 sts along one short side (pick up 3 sts in each contrast color stripe + 1 extra st at each side). Knit 9 rows garter st. Bind off in knitting. Work another edge the same way along the other short side. Turn bag inside out and seam the sides up to the edge.

Handles Use yarn of your color choice held double to knit 2 I-cords about 20 in / 50 cm long (see p. 57). Pull the handles through them and attach the handles. I have managed to find handles that can be covered by I-cord. If you can't find something similar, you can make handles of I-cord, sewing them securely at the top edge. You can make the handles extra sturdy by pulling thick clothesline cord through the I-cords.

hanna

I learned short-rows in 3rd grade, and I've used it in several designs in this book. Short-rows in garter stitch have the neat advantage that you don't have to hide the holes that usually appear at the turning points; they become next to invisible.

I also love the look of stripes, but I'm generally not very comfortable with them. Whenever I wear striped sweaters, I tend to feel like I've been sliced. In this set of gauntlets, cap and pouch, I've used short-row shaping which interplays in an interesting way with the stripes. The candy colors are given a more adult feel set off with gray, and the fact that the stripes are so thin makes Hanna a candidate for my own wardrobe.

Level of Difficulty   Intermediate

Sizes

Cap   Women's SM (ML)

Head circumference   20 (22¾) in

51 (58) cm

Gauntlets Length   10¾ in / 27 cm

Circumference up to   8 (9¾) in

20 (25) cm

Bag   5¼ × 6 in / 13 × 15 cm

Materials   Silky Wool

1 skein each of main color (MC), Contrast color (CC) 1, and contrast color 2 is enough for all 3 projects. If you want to make the items in a single color, you'll need 1 skein for the cap and 1–2 skeins for the gauntlets.

Needles   US size 6 / 4 mm

Gauge   22 sts × 44 rows in garter st = 4 × 4 in / 10 × 10 cm.

Adjust needle size to obtain gauge if necessary.

Garter st is very flexible; you can easily adjust sizing by knitting with smaller needles for a smaller size and larger needles for larger size.

Stripe sequence for gauntlets and cap

* 1 ridge CC 1, 1 ridge MC, 1 ridge CC 2, 1 ridge MC; repeat from *.

1 ridge = 2 rows. For nice looking edges when changing color, see page 47).

Gauntlets

Left gauntlet: With MC, cast on 60 sts, knit 1 row, and then work in stripe sequence above. All ridges begin at the top of the sleeve. Immediately begin short row shaping for arm.

Size SM: Knit 26 sts; turn and knit back. Knit 30 sts; turn and knit back. Knit 34 sts; turn and knit back.

Size ML: Knit 10 sts; turn and knit back. Knit 14 sts; turn and knit back. Continue the same way, with

4 more sts each time until the last row (knit with CC 2) has 34 sts.

Both sizes: Knit across all sts on row. When there are 26 ridges for the hand (left side of the piece), begin working thumb gusset (CC 1): Knit until 8 sts remain. You are now at the top edge of thumb gusset; short rows for thumb gusset begin here.

Thumb gusset: Knit 4 sts; turn and knit back. Knit 6 sts; turn and knit back. Continue the same way, with each row from top edge of thumb gusset 2 sts longer until you have worked 14 sts; turn and knit back. Now you are at the center ridge and can begin the other side of thumb gusset, reversing shaping: knit 12 sts; turn and knit back. Knit 10 sts; turn and knit back, *etc.*, until you have worked 4 sts; turn and knit back. Knit 52 sts. The thumb gusset is finished and you are now at the top edge of the gauntlet.

Continue striping (the next stripe is a CC) over entire row (60 sts). After 9 ridges from thumb gusset, work in short rows, reversing shaping: knit 34 sts; turn and knit back. Knit 30 sts; turn and knit back. Continue the same way with 4 fewer sts each time until the final row (knit in CC 1) of 10 sts. Knit 1 ridge with MC and then 1 ridge with CC 2. Leave the sts on the the needle and, using a 20 in / 50 cm strand of MC, graft seam or bind off in MC and sew seam.

Right gauntlet: Work as for left gauntlet, reversing shaping (there will be a 1 ridge difference so that the colors will match). Knit 1 row with MC and then shape arm with short rows. Work thumb gusset when there are 10 ridges on the hand and, when there are 25 ridges after thumb gusset, shape arm and end with 1 ridge in MC and then 1 ridge with CC 2; seam as for left gauntlet.

Cap

With CC 1, cast on 45 sts and knit 1 row (1st ridge of striping). Continue in stripe sequence above, beginning each ridge at lower edge of cap. Knit garter st short rows as follows: * Knit until 1 st remains; turn

and knit back. Work the following 11 (15) ridges each 1 st shorter than previous ridge. On the next ridge (CC), knit across all sts. Work the next 11 (15) ridges, reversing shaping until there are a total of 34 (30) sts; turn and knit back. Now work the following rows 1 st longer than the previous row until you are once again knitting over all sts across (CC). Repeat from * 3 times (= a total of 4 sections). Leave the sts on the needle and, using a 20 in / 50 cm strand of MC, graft sts or bind off in MC and sew seam. Fold up 3–5 sts along lower edge (whatever suits you) and sew neatly to WS.

Bag

For the modular technique, each square is worked in 2-row color stripes of garter st. Slip the first st of each row purlwise with yarn in front so that it will be easier to pick up and knit sts along the edge. The first modules are worked separately and then others are joined during knitting. Catch tails as you knit so that you won't have to weave in so many after you finish (see next page).

Free module

With MC, cast on 30 sts and knit 1 row, placing a marker at center (15 sts on each side).

Row 1, CC: Knit to 2 sts before marker, ssk, slip marker, k2tog, knit remaining sts = 28 sts. Knit next row.

Row 3, MC: Work as for row 1 = 26 sts. Knit next row.

Continue in this manner until 4 sts remain.

Next row: Ssk, remove marker, k2tog. Knit next row.

Last row: K2tog. Cut yarn.

Make another square the same way.

Knit-joined modules

With MC, pick up and knit 15 sts along one cast-on edge of a module and then another 15 sts along cast-on edge of second module. Knit 1 row, placing a marker at center (15 sts on each side). Knit a square as for free modules.

Knit 2 free modules with MC and CC 1.
Work 2 joined modules with MC and CC 2.

Do not cut yarn on the last module. Use working yarn to pick up and knit 30 sts along one side and knit 9 rows garter st. Bind off in knitting on RS but do not cut yarn. Use working yarn to pick up and knit 30 sts along each of the remaining 3 sides. Knit 1 row and cut yarn.

Knit the second half of the bag as for the first but do not cut yarn when you have finished the last row around the three sides. Place back and front pieces so right sides are facing outwards and use three-needle bind-off to join pieces. The finishing will be extra nice if you bind off in k1, p1 ribbing. Do not cut yarn but use working yarn to pick up and knit 4 sts along side of the top edge to knit an I-cord (see page 57) 32–40 in / 80–100 cm long or desired length. In the same way, pick up and knit an I-cord on the other side but make it only 3 in / 7.5 cm long. Fold the cord in half and attach the end on WS.

Changing colors

Always change colors on RS.

Bring the new color up behind the old throughout for a smoother edge and to facilitate finishing.

When there are several rows between stripes of the same color, as in Hanna, I recommend that you "catch" the contrast color from the stripe below whenever you start to knit with the main color. That way the color that is carried along the side will be hidden.

The photo also shows how the working yarn from the last knitted stripe is left at the front of the work.

asta

These attractive wristwarmers are the perfect introduction to lace patterns. They are worked in garter stitch, which makes them very flexible, so size won't be an issue. The "look-what-*I've*-done factor" is achieved by the simple but elegant lace edging.

This is my version of Annemor Sundbø's ping-pong wristwarmers, and I've added a pretty neckwarmer, a cell phone pouch and a case for your glasses for good measure. Apart from the neckwarmer, which requires intermediate knitting skills, this is, along with Randi, probably the easiest design in the book.

Level of Difficulty	Easy
	(Neckwarmer is Intermediate)
Materials	Silky Wool 1 skein
	5 buttons, ⅜ in / 1 cm diameter
	for neck warmer
Needles	US size 2 / 3 mm
Gauge	22 sts × 44 rows in garter stitch =
	4 × 4 in / 10 × 10 cm.

Adjust needle size to obtain gauge if necessary.

Wrist Warmers (make both alike)
Cast on 22 sts and work in garter stitch. Knit 1 row and then begin sawtooth edging:
* Knit until 2 sts remain, yo, k2 = 23 sts; turn and knit back.
Knit until 2 sts remain, yo, k2 = 24 sts; turn and knit back.
Knit until 2 sts remain, yo, k2 = 25 sts. On the next row, bind off the first 3 sts and then knit remaining sts across.

You are now back at the original number of sts (22). Repeat from * until wrist warmer goes around your wrist. It is better to have the piece a little too short than too long. The cuff will fit better if is a little tight. The cuff shown has 11 pattern repeats. Graft the live stitches to the cast-on row or bind off and graft bound-off and cast-on rows.

Cell phone pouch
Work as for wrist warmers—8 repeats should be enough to fit. Seam side and then straight edge for the bottom. Knit an I-cord about 24 in / 60 cm long (see page 57). Sew cord securely at each side of the sawtooth edging.

Glasses Case (see photo next spread)
Cast on 35 sts and work as for wrist warmers for 10 repeats. Seam side and then straight edge for the bottom.

Neck warmer

The neck warmer measures 13½ in / 34 cm when buttoned, but garter st is very flexible so the piece will easily fit a neck up to 15¾ in / 40 cm. If you want a larger size, add a repeat at center back and work 6 repeats instead of 5. You could even add a repeat at each side inside the button edge at the front. Each repeat adds about ¾ in / 2 cm.

Cast on 30 sts and work in garter st. Knit 7 rows = 4 garter ridges on RS for buttonband.

On the next row, cast on 5 new sts at the end of the row (which will be the sawtooth edge of the neckwarmer) and then knit 1 row back. Work the sawtooth edging as for wrist warmers. Keep in mind that you can only count the sts between the repeats. Work 2 repeats. Now begin shaping lower edge *while continuing the sawtooth edging throughout:* Work k2tog at beginning of *every other row* 3 times (= 1 repeat) and then k3tog at beginning of *every other row* 6 times (= 2 repeats) = 20 sts remain. Work 2 repeats without shaping lower edge.

Now increase at the lower edge by working k1, p1, k1 in the first st of *every other row* 6 times = 32 sts. Work 5 repeats without shaping lower edge.

Now decrease at lower edge with k3tog at beginning of *every other row* 6 times = 20 sts. Work 2 repeats without shaping.

Next, increase at lower edge by working k1, p1, k1 in first st of *every other row* 6 times and k1, p1 in first st of *every other row* 3 times = 35 sts. Work 2 repeats without shaping lower edge, but, *on the last row of the final sawtooth,* bind off the 3 sts of sawtooth pattern + 5 sts so that 30 sts remain.

Work these as buttonhole band: Continue in garter st. After 2 garter ridges, make buttonholes: k6, *yo, k2tog, k3; repeat from * across row = 5 buttonholes. Work until the buttonhole band has a total of 4 garter ridges and then bind off. Sew on buttons.

randi

Who would believe it, but yes, it is all garter stitch! Working with three colors ensures that the color you need to knit with next will be on the side where it should be. No shaping, minimal finishing, as easy as can be. When you have finished the scarf, there should be enough yarn left for the wristwarmers. Or the headband. Or both. Then you can start over with another color combination.

Apart from Randi being a playful design, the name itself is a play on words, even if that probably escapes most English-speaking people: The Swedish word "randig" actually means striped.

Level of Difficulty   Easy

Sizes
Scarf   9¾ × 59 in / 25 × 150 cm
Wrist warmers   4 in / 10 cm long

Materials   Silky Wool

2 skeins each of 3 colors (main color MC and contrast colors CC 1 and 2); leftovers from the scarf are enough for the wrist warmers and hairband

Needles   US sizes 4 and 32-in circular 7 / 3.5 mm and 80 cm circular 4.5 mm

Gauge   20 sts in garter st on larger needles = 4 in / 10 cm.
23 sts in garter st on smaller needles = 4 in / 10 cm.

Adjust needle sizes to obtain gauge if necessary.

Note Colors are changed on every row but, because you are working with three colors, the next color in the sequence will always hang at the correct side. In this way, you don't have to cut and reattach yarns. Always bring the new color up behind the old color.

Scarf

With circular needle and MC, cast on 300 sts and work in garter st and one-row stripes as follows: * knit 1 row with MC, 1 row with CC 1 and 1 row with CC 2. Repeat from * throughout. Work in pattern for 9¾ in / 25 cm. End with 1 row MC and then bind off loosely with MC. *Fringe:* Cut 2 strands of each color. 16 in / 40 cm long. Fold strands twice and then pull through each dark brown stripe (see drawing below).

Wrist Warmers (make both alike)

With smaller needles and MC, cast on 22 sts and work in garter st and one-row striping as for scarf. Work until piece fits snugly around your wrist, about 6–7 in / 15–18 cm. End with 1 row MC and then bind off loosely with MC. Seam by grafting as invisibly as possible.

Hairband

With smaller needles and MC, cast on 11 sts and work in garter st and one-row striping as for scarf. On the 5th stripe with MC, work k1, p1, k1 in the outermost st on each side = 15 sts. Knit until strip measures about 15 in / 38 cm long. On the next MC row, work a double dec at each side = 11 sts. Work without further shaping until hairband fits around your head. End with 1 row MC and then bind off loosely with MC. Seam by grafting as invisibly as possible.

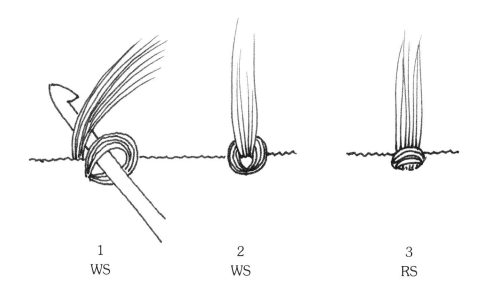

1
WS

2
WS

3
RS

tina

Sometimes I like to go a little crazy, and here's one example: I played with a different shape for a tea cozy, and ended up with two variations; one that ties over the lid, and one that buttons onto the knob of the lid. Then I went all out with I-cord decorations. You can leave them out for a more strict design, or you can choose even wilder colors than I did.

 The bottom of the tea cozy is round, and I turned a larger version of it into hot pads (see the next spread). Both are made with Silky Wool held double. And yes, that's my own, frequently used, tea mug beside the pot. Tea is, in my case, "designer fuel".

Level of Difficulty Intermediate

Sizes S (M) L

 (M fits a standard 1.2 liter / quart teapot)

Materials Silky Wool 2 skeins

 Remnants of Bambool or Silky Wool in 3 colors for embellishments

Needles US size 7 / 4.5 mm

 Crochet hook US size G / 4.5 mm for provisional cast-on

Gauge 18 sts × 36 rows in garter st with yarn held double = 4 × 4 in / 10 × 10 cm.

Adjust needle size to obtain gauge if necessary.

Tea Cozy

Half of the cozy With yarn held double, cast on 20 (24) 28 sts and knit 4 (3) 2 garter ridges = 7 (5) 3 rows.

Begin garter stitch short rows: * Knit until 3 (4) 5 sts remain; turn and knit back until 3 (4) 5 sts remain; turn and knit next row until 3 (4) 5 sts remain; turn and knit next row with 3 (4) 5 fewer sts (there are 8 sts between the last 2 turning points); turn and complete row. Knit 1 row across all sts *. This short row sequence represents one garter ridge at the edges.

Work 4 garter ridges followed by the short row sequence (*–*). Repeat this 3 (4) 5 times and end with the short row sequence and 4 (3) 2 garter ridges = 24 (27) 30 garter ridges. Bind off. Make another piece the same way.

Top: With yarn held double, pick up and knit 24 (27) 30 sts along one side (1 st in each "knot" along garter stitch edge = 1 st in each ridge). Work in garter st. When there are 4 ridges, decrease evenly spaced across row: * K2tog, k1; repeat from * = 16 (18) 20 sts.

Knit 1 row and then decrease: * k2tog; repeat from * = 8 (9) 10 sts.

Version that ties over the teapot lid:

Knit 20 ridges and then increase 1 st at each side on every other row 2 times = 12 (13) 14 sts. Knit 2 rows

and then work k2tog at the beginning of every row until no sts remain.

Version that buttons onto the teapot lid:

Knit 2 ridges. *Next row:* Bind off the center 4 (5) 6 sts; complete row. On the next row, cast on 4 (5) 6 new sts over the bound-off ones. Knit 4 rows and then work k2tog at the beginning of *every* row until no sts remain.

Make other half of tea cozy the same way.

Bottom: With yarn held double, cast on 8 (9) 10 sts and knit 1 row. Now begin working short rows: knit 1; turn and knit back. Knit 2; turn and knit back. Continue the same way with 1 more st on each short row until you knit across all the sts; turn and knit back. This completes 1 section. Knit a total of 6 sections the same way. Leave a 12-inch / 30 cm tail and graft the live sts to the cast-on edge or bind off and use mattress st to seam the edges.

Finishing

Securely sew both parts of the body to the bottom, matching ridge to ridge.

Embellish with randomly placed I-cords (see next page) knit in 3 colors of Bambool or Silky Wool used double. I recommend I-cords about 2–3 in / 5–7 cm long.

On the Dark brown tea cosy I've sewn them into loops placed near each other in groups of two or three. On the golden tea cozy I've knitted pairs of I-cord close to each other and tied them into knots.

Hot pads

With waste yarn and crochet hook, make a crochet provisional cast-on of 15 sts. With working yarn held double, knit 15 sts (1 row) and then begin short rows: k2; turn and knit back. Knit 3; turn and knit back. Continue the same way with 1 more st on each short row until you knit across all the sts; turn and knit back. This forms 1 section. Repeat until there are a total of 6 sections. At end of last section, leave a 12 in / 30 cm tail for grafting. Unpick the crochet cast-on and then use Kitchener st to graft first and last rows.

Pick up 3 sts along the edge and knit a 3 in / 8 cm I-cord, form a loop, and sew it securely at point where sts were picked up.

Knitting I-cords

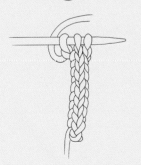

With 2 double pointed needles, cast on 4 sts: * k4, do not turn work; instead, slide sts to front of left needle and knit them. Repeat from * throughout. When I-cord reaches desired length, cut yarn and pull tail through sts.

You can also pick up sts directly from the work (as on the Tina teacozy), or along an edge (as for the loop on the hot pads above) and knit the I-cord onto the piece.

malin

Whyever is this type of headgear called a smoke ring? This lovely version is worked in a pretty 19th century lace pattern known, at least in Sweden, as an owlet moth pattern. It is worked on every row, so the whole thing is knitted in the round. Shaping is done by changing to smaller needles as you go. The result is both flattering and functional.

In the photos, we've combined Malin with the Baby Llama sweater Cipher from The Out of the Blue Collection. Nice match, if I may say so myself.

repeat 22 sts

Level of Difficulty   Fairly easy
Size
   Width at top edge   21¾ in / 55 cm
   Width at lower edge   27½ in / 70 cm
   Length   19¾ in / 50 cm
Materials   Silky Wool 2 skeins
Needles   16-in / 40 cm circulars US sizes 6, 7, and 8 / 4, 4.5, and 5 mm
Gauge   24 sts in pattern on needles US 6 / 4 mm = 4 in / 10 cm.
Adjust needle sizes to obtain gauge if necessary.

With circular US size 8 / 5 mm, cast on 132 sts and join, being careful not to twist cast-on row. Knit 1 row and then work in pattern following chart. Use US 8 / 5 mm needles for 6 in / 15 cm; work another 6 in / 15 cm with US 7 / 4.5 mm needles, and then continue with US 6 / 4 mm. When piece measures 19¾ in / 50 cm, after a complete repeat, turn work inside out and work 4 rows in stockinette (purls will be on RS). Bind off and weave in tail neatly so it won't show on outside.

Technical information

The information below is not a list of absolutes but simply explains the techniques I have used for these patterns. I find that working in this manner makes the finishing easier and gives a more beautiful result. Feel free to use whichever techniques you prefer.

Casting On

Long-tail or continental cast-on

I normally use the long-tail or continental cast-on. It has one side which looks more refined than the other. The first row is worked on the wrong side so that the nicer-looking edge will show on the right side. That is also why all the ribbings have an odd number of rows. Casting on over two needles held together will make the cast-on row more elastic.

Crochet cast-on (provisional cast-on)

With waste yarn, crochet a chain several stitches lon-

ger than the number of stitches needed. Pick up stitches in the back loops of the chain. Afterwards the crochet chain can easily be unraveled and the stitches picked up for  knitting. Note that when you knit in the other direction, the new stitches will be placed between the old stitches, and you will lose ½ stitch at each side.

Knitted cast-on

Start with a loop or the first st on left needle. Knit into st, but leave the stitch on the left needle. Turn the new stitch and place it on the left needle so that it sits on the needle as a knit 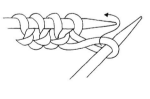 stitch. Repeat, knitting 1 st into first st on left needle and then placing new st on left needle.

Increases

I usually increase using a right lifted increase (RLI) at the beginning of a row, and a left lifted increase (LLI) at the end. For increases spaced across a row or in the pattern, I usually use M1 (lift the running thread between 2 sts and knit into back loop). Purl into the back loop for M1p.

Decreases

Decrease within the edge stitches by working a k2tog at the beginning of a row and ssk at the end of a row unless otherwise specified. It is easier to decrease on the smooth side of the work irregardless of whether it is the right or wrong side.

Ssk: slip 2 sts as if to knit, one at a time. Knit them together through back loops. Slipping the stitches will turn them so that, when you knit them together through the back loops, they will not be twisted (a mirror image of k2tog). *Sssk* is worked in the same manner, but slipping 3 sts, and mirrors k3tog.

Stitches on holder

Binding off using waste yarn makes for easier blocking. When picking up the stitches again, just unravel the bound-off edge.

Short-rows, wrap and turn (W&T)

When working short-rows, you turn the work before reaching the end of the row, thereby adding two rows across a section of the work. In most instructions, I shape the shoulders with short rows without wrapping, which will most often work beatifully if you tighten the working yarn before turning and working back. If you are not satisfied with the result you can wrap at each turn as follows:

Knit side

Work until the turning point; with the yarn in back, slip the next stitch as if to  purl. Bring the yarn to the front of the piece and slip the stitch back to the left needle. Turn the piece and work back.

On the following row, when you reach the wrapped  stitch, insert the needle under the wrap and into the front of the stitch as shown, and knit them together.

Purl side

Work until the turning point; with the yarn in front, slip the next stitch as if to purl.  Bring the yarn to the back of the piece and slip the stitch back to the left needle. Turn the piece and work back.

On the following row, when you reach the wrapped 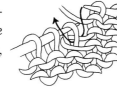 stitch, insert the needle under the wrap and into the back of the stitch as shown, and purl them together.

Three-needle bind-off, knitting shoulders together

Place pieces with right sides facing each other and needles pointing in the same direction. K2tog (1 st from each needle), repeat this and pass the first stitch over the second. Continue in this manner, knitting one st from each needle and binding off as usual.

Blocking

Always block pieces before finishing. This will make the job of finishing easier, even out your knitting and you will get a better result.

Seams

Most seams will look their best if grafted together from the right side, though backstitching inside the edge stitch will do for most side and sleeve seams. I recommend that you at least graft in all the most visible places, such as the ribbing, edges and collars. Set-in sleeves need the extra stability of backstitching.

Vertical grafting on stockinette *Vertical grafting on reverse stockinette* *Vertical grafting on garter stitch*

When knitting sweaters with straight armholes in stockinette stitch, end the sleeves with a knit row from the wrong side and then bind off. The knit ridge will create a smoother transition between sleeve and body.

Attaching sleeve using grafting

Weaving in ends

When knitting a garment with several colors, I recommend that you weave in the ends as you knit. It is easy to do and you won't have as many tails to weave in when the piece is finished.

Place the tail to be woven in over the index finger and then place the working yarn over both the index and middle fingers (near the tip of the fingernails). * With needle over the tail on the index finger, catch the working yarn and complete the stitch. Next, go under the tail on the index finger, catch the working yarn and complete the stitch. Repeat from * 2–3 times and the tail is secured. You can also use this technique for joining in new colors. Note that this may not work if you throw the yarn with your right hand.

Abbreviations

ch	chain
cm	centimeter(s)
cn	cable needle
in	inch(es)
inc	increase
k	knit
k2tog	knit 2 sts together
k3tog	knit 3 sts together
LC	Left Cable
LLI	Left Lifted Increase
M1	Make 1: lift the running thread between 2 sts and knit into back loop
M1p	Make 1 purl: lift the running thread between 2 sts and purl into back loop
mm	millimeter(s)
p	purl
p2tog	purl 2 sts together
pm	place marker
RC	Right Cable
RLI	Right Lifted Increase
RS	Right Side
s2kp2	slip 2 as if to knit together, k1, pass the 2 slipped sts over
sc	single crochet
sk2p	slip 1 as if to knit, k2tog, pass the slipped st over
sl	slip(ping)
slm	slip marker
ssk	slip, slip, knit sts tog through back loops
sssk	slip, slip, slip, knit the 3 slipped sts together through back loops
st(s)	stitch(es)
tbl	through back loop(s)
tog	together
W&T	Wrap and Turn (see Short-rows, p. 60)
WS	Wrong Side
wyib	with yarn in back
wyif	with yarn in front
yo	yarn over

Reading charts

A chart is like a map of a pattern. Every square in the chart equals a stitch of knitting. A horizontal row corresponds to a row of knitting and a vertical row is a straight line of stitches, one over the other.

The chart shows how a pattern looks on the right side. The same symbol can mean a stitch is worked differently on the right and wrong sides. The symbols are explained in the list on p. 63.

The right side rows are odd-numbered and are read from right to left; wrong side rows are read from left to right. In circular knitting, all rows are read from right to left.

If a pattern consists of a set of stitches or "repeat" which is to be worked several times, begin working at the marker for row 1, or, as indicated in some instructions, at a size marker, and work until the beginning of the repeat. The repeat is then worked the number of times indicated or as many times as possible. The row is finished by working to the end of the chart or until the stitches are used up. Unless otherwise indicated, all rows are repeated for the entire length. The size marker points to a square that is usually worked as an edge stitch regardless of what the chart shows. Motif placement is explained in the text.

In some patterns, the stitch count can vary from row to row. For those patterns, the chart is drawn so that the largest number of stitches can be shown. On rows with fewer stitches, black squares are inserted so that stitches which are worked directly above each other can be shown that way on the chart. These black squares have no meaning for the knitting! When you come to a black square on the chart, skip it and go to the next square that is not black and work it as indicated.

Chart symbols

☐	k on RS, p on WS	╱	k2tog on RS
⊡	p on RS, k on WS	╲	ssk on RS
✛	k on RS, k on WS	╲.	k2tog on WS
■	no stitch	╱.	ssk on WS
○	yo	⋏	k3tog
⅄	right lifted increase see p. 16	⋋	s2kp
⅄	left lifted increase see p. 16	⋀	s2kp2

2/2 Right Cable: slip 2 sts to cn, hold to back, k2; k2 from cn

2/2 Left Cable: slip 2 sts to cn, hold to front, k2; k2 from cn

2/2 Right Purl Cable: slip 2 sts to cn, hold to back, k2; p2 from cn

2/2 Left Purl Cable: slip 2 sts to cn, hold to front, p2; k2 from cn

3/3 Right Cable: slip 3 sts to cn, hold to back, k3; k3 from cn

3/3 Left Cable: slip 3 sts to cn, hold to front, k3; k3 from cn

Distributors:

USA:
Euro Yarns (a division of KFI)
315 Bayview Avenue
Amityville
New York
USA
NY11701
Tel: 001 516 546 3600
Fax: 001 516 546 6871
www.knittingfever.com

CANADA:
Nova Yarn Ltd
155 Martin Ross Avenue
Unit 3
Toronto
Ontario M3J 2L9
CANADA
Tel: 001 416 736 6111
Fax: 001 416 736 6112
www.novayarn.com

In the near future, Elsebeth Lavold Designer's Choice yarns and books will be available in Europe, Australia, and Asia. Please email admin@knittingfever.com for more information about purchasing our yarns and fine designs in your country.